The Bee Telephone

Poems by

Jane Wiseman

Copyright by Jane Wiseman
2024

Choeofpleirn Press, LLC

All rights reserved.
This book may not be reproduced, in whole or in part, including illustrations, in any form for any purposes other than scholarly discussion or reviewing, without written permission from the publishers.

Although the author and publisher have made every effort to ensure that the information in this book was correct at press time, the author and publisher do not assume and hereby disclaim any liability to any party for any loss, damage, or disruption caused by errors or omissions, whether such errors or omissions result from negligence, accident,
or any other cause.

Without in any way limiting the author's and publisher's exclusive rights under copyright, any use of this publication to "train" or develop generative artificial intelligence (AI) technologies is expressly prohibited. The author and publisher reserve all rights to license uses of this work for generative AI training and development
of machine learning language models.

ISBN:
(print) 979-8-9904058-7-5
(digital) 979-8-9911790-1-0

Jane Wiseman's stunning debut brims with wit and lyrical invention. In poems musical and skillfully layered, rebellious dandelions defy "the grudging neighbor" wielding "pique and poison" with "the gold force of their flame." In "Penelope, Exasperated," the famously patient wife abandons her loom (and overdue Ulysses); in another, the Devil promises to "dance you widdershins/until the blood cock crows." The essential drive of the book, for me, shows itself in the marvelous title poem in which "otherworldly" bees enchant us with sacred and mysterious "barbed texts/scoured in honey, scribed in wax."

Amy Beeder,
author of *And So Wax Was Made & Also Honey* (Tupelo Press),
Burn the Field (Carnegie Mellon Poetry),
Now Make an Altar (Carnegie Mellon Poetry)

Jane Wiseman's *The Bee Telephone* is a tour de force of language and image. These poems know no bounds, taking the reader from the intimate workings of insects' lives to the chiming of the universe. Wiseman is a scholar of medieval and renaissance literature - and it shows in her incantatory rhythm and language. Her voice is absolutely unique, but strong and sure as she conjures an entire world in each poem. And the overarching theme here seems to be beauty– sometimes harsh or disturbing but always glorious.

Joanie McLean,
author of *Like Wind Into Air*, Redhawk Publications

What is it like to swim in words and rise from the water with new eyes? Jane Wiseman plunges us into waters where words are like rip tides taking us places that we never imagined and only slowly wake to, as she tells us about "lying at the verge of the/green-gray Atlantic, oh, seven,/or eight years old, trailing over/ the lip of the Continent, swaddled/ in the lap of warm sand." How Wiseman sees the world and herself in it unfolds poem by poem as she asks of us, her readers, to see abundance. Everything we glean here is akin to the nectar that bees discover from flower to flower in the form of a poem, the poems themselves nourishment for our minds.

Iris Tillman Hill,
author of *All this Happened Long Ago*, Main St. Rag Press

The Bee Telephone iv

For my family—*sine qua non*

The Bee Telephone vi

Table of Contents

The Bee Telephone	1
The Largest Intact Caldera on the Continent	2
The Dandelion Despised	3
Fool's Spring	4
Mericarp	5
Glyph	7
The comet, that hairy star	8
Slow Waking	9
Penelope, Exasperated	10
Coming soon to skies near you	11
Bitter Gourd	13
Breughel and Babel	14
CHIME	15
Hard Freeze in the North	16
Meditation in Formic	17
Drawing from a Plaster Cast	18
Sell your soul to the Devil at the crossroads	19
The Faux-Bougereau over the Square Grand	20
The morning you drove me to the station	22
The Trip Down	23
Tripes à la Mode de Caen	24
A Conventicle of Magpies	25
I'm talking good news	26
The mourning dove sounds like gone	28
Mown	29
Rebellion of the Things	30
Garden of Earthly Delights	31
In Memory, the Woodthrush	32
Salute to the Bluebird Café	33
Ornithomancer	34
The gazelle springing	35
Acknowledgments	37
About the Poet	39
Judge's Comments	41

The Bee Telephone viii

The Bee Telephone
Hayes Arboretum, Richmond, Indiana

On their side of the glassed-in wall
they go about whatever other-worldly thing
they do. On our side, too, we hum and buzz.
Everything's commotion, mothers, children,
strollers, the occasional dad. Kids make a beeline
for the red phone. In a distant universe,
pollen-laden devotees dance to the sun.
A static hiss from a different hive. The burr,
the sizzle of an alien tribe, barbed texts
scoured in honey, scribed in wax.

The Largest Intact Caldera on the Continent

I'd like to see them try, she says.
Perhaps they thought her dormant.
That tectonic shift we witnessed. Was it
in the slide of shoulder, mere suggestion
of the tilt of head, as if the surface tension
of the magma chamber rippled? Forces reft
from deep to surface. Calenture profound,
heating the null of atmosphere to charged.
The air crackles. Dogs howl.
Swimming pools suck down to geyser up
in chunks of pale green painted concrete.
Fault lines widen and go rogue.

A benign edenic bowl, once a cinder cone
to rival Kilimanjaro. Cattle graze the green slopes
            now.
Red-clad Maasai chivvy them into thorn-brush
            closures,
flicking their placid flanks with split, slippery
            wands.

The Dandelion Despised

Though the grudging neighbor eyes my yard,
urges her toxic applications and her remedies,
these bright faces stud the grass, her own sour
      face
outfaced, dominion rising, ragged of the earth.
Day wanes. Beneath the moon, a transformation.
Monarch crowns, sturdy on their scapes, wisp out
into blowballs, whisper defiance into pale strands.
Milk-veins leak across flashpoint borders, toothed
      leaves
throw down. The wind their servant rushes the clocks
on the pulse of the universe, populates its empire
with their kind. She who wields pique and poison
cannot halt their march. The gold force of their
      flame.

Fool's Spring

"The weather out there is just plain mean."

A deceit of lapwings, peewits,
pyewipes, dotterels wedged
beneath a moon-cold night.
The witches are flying.
Their squadrons and columns
cut the streaks of cloud.
Bog-plants rise and listen:
sabbatia, cranberry, yellow-eyed grass,
the benign with the carnivorous.
All embed, attend in the red chill
of their matted sphagnum,
the schwingmoor quaking
over its vast spread,
taking for set truth the lie
that all this lying spills
into cold enormity. Vile,
the deception. Profligate,
the destruction, buds cased
in ice, their promise stunted,
dry sticks rubbing together,
quag clatter, mere clacking.

Mericarp

Dry season, dry fruit,
a single seed enflorescing
out of many.

Here's the public-facing petal, here's
the flower.

Merry dance, the flash and fillip
of masked ball, eyes meeting, eyes
aslant, concealing and revealing
cryptic meat inside the rind,
unlovely, shrunken, unshriven.

Carp at it. Convict it of hiding.
Lodge it underfoot. A magpie,
a vole seizes on it, squirrels it
grieving and greeting, nests it
in roost, in burrow.

Burrow it underground, under skin,
undercroft of the cruel court. Let it
in winter lie down.

In springtime, it greens out fine,
the flaunting petal, fluting to flower,
afloat, tossing across silk summer. That,
let everyone gape at, everyone greet.

Stroke it and court it. In autumn,
fickle suitor, turn away. In autumn,
all edges begin their wilt; these too
will brittle and brown.

But the shattering: ballistic husk
of touch-me-not, fled fierce
out of slit rough prison
to chill blue air.

Glyph

Feel the words slip out, slide past the tongue,
poise on the lips. Words launch themselves;
mysteriously drip off the tips of fingers; roll,
pearl by pearl, out through the tubes of pens.
Tick at the ends of keys.

The telescope, the microscope of language.

Unship the spyglass from its brass mountings.
Blunder along the path, follow til it ends
at the end of the map, the rift where the world
splinters to syllable, grapheme, symbol without sign.

The comet, that hairy star

has come to scorch the skies above the land.
It is a sign. The sun has dulled to red,
moves in, swings low on a low horizon, and
that paragon rides regnant overhead,
portent to the baked earth, omen to
destroy. Her blowback is a head of seed,
a crown of sparks. She vibrates, sforzando.
We listen for her thrumming, in our need
attuned to turnings of a burdened sphere,
to keening wind and to the scud across
the hardpan. Tasks of hand, of eye, of ear
have dwindled now to these: To note our loss.
Bear witness to the signs we mourn too late,
small and on a dying planet. Wait.

Slow Waking

Like lying at the verge of the
green-gray Atlantic, oh, seven,
eight years old, trailing over
the lip of the Continent, swaddled
in the lap of warm sand. Or as if
I'm so small a giant hand holds me
lightly against the dawn hum
of the recomposing self. Or like
huddling knees to skinny chest
beneath some overhang while
all around a humid dripping,
a rich, a vegetative mist rises
in the velvet dark.

                       Then
this waking. A world mildewed,
sour rot, the future. Offer up
a coin to the dream-gods.
Strike a bargain. Promise
to light a candle, make sacrifice,
do every little favor for them,
anything so they ferry me back
in their veiled craft, deep, and
far enough under again.

Penelope, Exasperated

I have given you bread and salt.
You salted the furrows, you salted the wound.
You wound your way across the Adriatic
ten years to me, while I, wily, unraveled
this loom, turned into your maybe,
turn and return and turn again. Made me
bitter. Made me old. You, what may you gain?
Kill the suitors, hang the maids? What? What?
You know the secret of our bed. It suits you that
I wait. No. This time when you're gone, when
the weight of you is gone, I step onto the portico, and
Goddess, I hold up my hands. You, down at the port
with all your faithful hands. A sail stands in to harbor.
This time I'm done. No more understanding woman.
If you come back, know it, I'll be gone.

Don't think to moor in that same cove again.

Coming soon to skies near you

the asteroid Apophis, whiskering past.
Maybe I'll be dead by then. 2029. Maybe
I'll ride it out past the sun to the apogee
of that rock's orbit. Zero chance hitting us,
so they say.
Yet we're about to tinker with it.

Messing with the demonic. Apophis, aka Apep,
Egyptian god of chaos emanated umbilically
veiny and outraged from the navel of Ra.

Priests urge Ra, Assume cat-form. Clobber Apep!

Spit upon him.
Defile him with the left foot.
Take up a lance and smite him.
Fetter him.
Take up a knife and smite him some more.
Put fire upon him.

For further instructions, consult
The Book of the Overthrowing of Apep.

Not so fast.

rock-form Apophis
makes the Kessel Run in under twelve parsecs

Justice once shattered

out of its leaking innards
slithers doom.

Apophis, zipping by

in the dregs of the decade.

Bitter Gourd

The squirrels arrive, sizing up our pumpkin.
Cheeks bulging, they tidy the seeds in their thrift.
They've eaten a hole in the side, crawled within,
stripping the flesh away from the inside out.
The geese have veed up; warblers have abandoned.
Sunk sleeping to the stream's bed, bluegill, trout.
Newts laze the slack mud of the freezing pond.
One desiccated gourd, its striped skin split—
the crackling of the last leaf hanging on—
Who is the watcher? Who witnesses it?
Whether we stand at the window, together, alone,
moving beside us with its whisper, Death.
The air stills. Winter readies to sift in,
cover over the shame, the rot of life. Shut down.

Breughel and Babel

I went to Rome to see the wonders.
I made drawings there. The Coliseum,
monumental pride of the Caesars, ruined
now. I must not say this: Rome will have her fall.
Words of mine will get me taken, tortured, killed.
I'll draw a little wheel, and a man upon it.
Other men torment him there. I don't build in words.
In Rotterdam, the scholar's seen to it. Through him,
holy writ breathes out, our own tongue, on us.
Letters, the printer's art, make us to know it. But I.
I drew my tower.

Returned from that city, I drew another, and here's another.
They spiral up. Note how their arches lean on the diagonal.
They'll fall. Busy builders in their pride. Nimrod, his men.
The babble of language. Cisneros, Erasmus. Rome and
all its scholars. A stream of words spiraling toward
the heavens out of the bellies and mouths of men.
How it topples over, their edifice made of words. Mine's
built of good paint. I ground the colors myself. Here's
the wood I daubed it on. Wood crumbles. Paint fades.
My vanity's as great as theirs. God knows I know it.
But I made these towers. Here they are.

CHIME

The CHIME radio telescope has picked up intense periodic bursts of radio waves from a galaxy an almost incomprehensible distance from Earth, as evidenced by the signal-to-noise ratio.

*My heart bangs like a drum, propelling that
frail ship seven decades on. The once-clean
valves seize up. Spiky parts wear flat,
flat parts flatter. One day this machine
shuts down, the cadence of its bobbing rhymes
ceased*
                      The universe pulses, chimes
like a gong. Billions of light years from here,
the heartbeat of a distant galaxy
booms out its signal. What does it care
for small flapping sails? An FRB,
radio waves, the longest recorded bursts,
powerful, periodic. Throb of some neutron
star belling out to oceanic reaches
the big swells. Don't call it noise. Pattern.

Hard Freeze in the North

I feel myself unfurling like a flower,
dormant leaves nudging up from earth.
Sullen and grudging winter, lulled, ever
coaxed by stars, a star, the sway of the girth
of the planet, seeking a balance, finding true.
Zone by zone slow-motion explosion,
pedicel, florescence, rolling through
the latitudes. What if it's false, a con
to tease out flourishing? That tragedy, Lent.
The long night I should have expected,
the dying-back, the curse I should repent.
Here's the dark, cutting into the bud.
Every turn of the year, shouldn't I learn it,
lesson of ash? And every year I don't.

Meditation in Formic

What would I give,
those days crouched
in the field, grass prickling
my ankles above nylon
frilled cuffs of socks,
to watch, eye-level,
how they march,
dandelion their standard;
their determined sorties.
Each its votive crumb
for the queen. Each
communicating to each
the avoidance of hazard—
bridging a gap,
hummock to hummock,
a clamber of bodies.
Granivore mice thieving
the seed-haul from under
their very mandibles.
Some stoned bird,
ecstatic and anting.
At times famine.
Committing each one
each segmentation,
spiracle, petiole, gaster,
to the good of the tribe.
Genuflecting with each
geniculate antenna
to honor the glory
of the drop of rain,
its slow slide along
the green blade, mirror
upside down for sky.

Drawing from a Plaster Cast

Am I up to this? I don't think so. These lips
are faintly smiling. My lips, the ones
on my big sheet of paper, they're
faintly sneering. The lips of the plaster cast,
copy of a copy of a copy of some ancient Roman
woman or maybe was it a pretty man? Imagine her/him/they
standing still as the sculptor modeled them, hawked them
to a rich plebeian jumped-up from the countryside
for the peristyle of his new villa. The one with the fish mosaics
in the floor of the triclinium, now rubble. I think of the sculptor
roving the slums of Rome, easing between the leaning rickety
         insulae,
spotting some lovely half-starved woman/man/person.
Come with me. Have I got a job for you. Or perhaps
his model was enslaved, a Celt or maybe Greek.

No, if this body part, cruelly disembodied, belongs to the nose
I tried to draw last month, that means the model (long dead,
and the sculptor, and the rich patron) breathed Roman to the
         very core,
proud nose of a Roman, faint shadow of the shadow of a body,
         blood
once pounding through veins faintly blue beneath fine skin.
Flushing rosy, turning kissable these proud, these smiling lips.

Sell your soul to the Devil at the crossroads

Take up your pen and sign it. Poison's my ink.
At the place where three roads cross, at the stake,
      the wheel,
jangling toward you—what else could you think?—
harness, horses, cart. Tell me you feel
the hate of the crowd. Bite of the rope to bind,
iron of your chain. This night, let the moon
ride through rags of cloud. For me, find
a blood-spot heliotrope. And the white bone,
shape into the long flute. Play me home,
I'll sing you. I will dance you widdershins
until the blood-cock crow. Oh, now, come,
every singer's a sell-soul, the veil thins,
spirit layered with song. Pay up, pay the fare.
Blood-price at the crossroads. Meet me there.

The Faux-Bougereau over the Square Grand

Cheesecake sanitized as myth: How the art critic described the massive painting over my grandmother's parlor piano.

Pianoforte.
soft hard.

   Larger than life-sized. Semi-clad. Pursued by leering cupids reaching out to touch her more than ample flanks.

    the kind piano tuners won't touch

    too difficult to work with   so ornate

    So *gilded age—*

    nobody played it   nobody could

The tall brick Presbyterian household
of my grandmother. Nobody touched, nothing touched, the meat vegetable starch arranged on the Spode arranged on the massive mahogany table for Sunday-after-church lunch.

    She steps from the canvas, all a-quiver. Flees down the hills of Arcadie from touch of lustful Pan. Goddess help Your acolyte.

   She piteously to chaunge her shape
   the water nymphs besought.

The goat-god lunged to grope her, got a handful of reeds.
Had his will in the end.

      turned her

      tuned her from girl to music

      These old square grands. Antique dealers tell you,
      chop them up for firewood.

Not worth a thing.

Soft leather-covered hammers, not the harder felt.
Purer tone

muted notes charmed from

an iron-framed box

      over-strung   tense

      delicate fingers poised over

      ivory

      fleeting almost-ghostly

      touch

The morning you drove me to the station

you hurled them,
word after word riposte,
edges so jagged I threw up a shield,
labials I could wind about me.
Under the blows the shield did not crack.
The split fricatives, the grooved,
the onslaught, the assault.
At 30th Street Station sat silent three hours,
laminal, apical, retroflexed.
The train pulled out. Seven hours later,
struck dumb, I felt my way through the parking lot.
Home, I discovered I'd left my silk coat,
sibilants spilling in softening frails
from the overhead rack. No point in calling;
susurration headed for points mysterious,
further than hushing. Further than that.

The Trip Down

You didn't cut the rope in time,
so you followed me down. I saw
you didn't want it that way, I saw you
try to saw the last of the frayed
strands holding us together. Too late.
We plummeted. Together we fell.
It didn't take us long to reach the bottom.
It took too long. It took all the rest
of our lives. The smash-up was
terrific. We lay in a tangle looking up.
For an instant we wondered *what is this?*
An instant was all we had to understand,
to make out what, exactly, happened. It took
forever. It took us the rest of our lives.

Tripes à la Mode de Caen

Drain, wash, soak, blanch,
cut into one and a half inch squares
a kilo rumen reticulum omasum
what does it matter what he said or did
for my part I am terrified by fire
what does it matter that one afternoon when we
what does it matter then that nothing ever
Me miserum! certas habuit puer ille sagitta
really, what bosh what bunk what balony
uror, et in vacuo pectore regnat Amo
the burning of that barb as it withdraws
a draw-weight, can you believe it, one hundred pounds
about the size of a clenched fist, yes it is hollow
they taught me how to lay my body in the bow
sapwood and heartwood, yew is always best and yew
is fit for mourning think too that the only way
for clean removing is to push straight through
no arterial spray only this cold seeping

A Conventicle of Magpies

One for sorrow, two for mirth, sorrow sore
their fellow their felled.

Take tiding to sweep, circle and cycle.
Three be death. Four be birth.

Make berth upon stopped breath,
Barrow of earth.

Their vigilant eye. Five: silver. Six.
Though all that is glistering never be gold,

though the whole tittering shivers to sky,
though seven, your secret, girl, never be tolled,

they beak lamb's bowels, they bore
to the vitals of kind. Murther. Murtherer.

Eight, eat up cherries. Fright childer, scritch out.
Though you scath them and stanch them brood
    and flock,

nine to your lintel, ten to your branch,
eleven, your rooftree. Twelve o the clock.

They gather to mourn, gather feck and foul.
Pretty bird pretty bird gather all.

I'm talking good news

Henbane and hellebore, datura and may, all plants that sting and bite with their toothed and veiny leaves. Witchery and catchery, the sap that itches, crosshatching in stripes the unwary skin. I'm talking predator gooseneck loosestrife, the thug who sneaks, propagating by rhizome.

I'm talking Don't. I'm talking Don't.

Don't become complacent. The cockroach has nothing on them. When the asteroid came for triceratops and diplodicus, a thousand years of fernspike frolicked up and down the K/Pg Boundary.

I'm talking good news.

I'm talking close your windows, lock your doors. Here comes kudzu. The innocuous zucchini chaste beneath its leaf by day swells monstrous in the night. It beats down your door, menaces the dog, steals your changeling babies.

The Anthropocene Apocalypse. Good news. I'm talking Armageddon of mammals.

No Dark Cloud But Has Its Silver Lining shrieks the mandrake, ruptures from the earth cataclysmic, the muscular hydrostat of the Kingdom of Plants, creeper agnate invading the Dream of the Fisherman's Wife.

Be Sober. Be Vigilant. Our vegetable love will grow vaster than empires. Even the virus sends forth its tentacle. Seeking for whom it may devour.

Only perhaps the mouse survives, cowering in the cornerboard, overlooked, unsung, ensuring the future of hanta and buboe, lassa and flea.

The mourning dove sounds like gone

moans under the eaves of this house I'm leaving,
more spirit maybe than bird, the spirit
of abandoned places dismantled.
How best to say good riddance now get out.

That bird sounds reproach, the tug of an old rot,
a treachery, a sawing dissolution.
The sheen of its feathers underneath the gray.
The throb of its call, a grief mere illusion.

Only instinct, only some unsettled motion,
flurry of its wings, a scrabbling against the sill.
There's a stale smell in this house, lingering
long after stuff is packed off to Goodwill,

some kind of hanging on, stubborn, until
the last stick of it's hauled to the dump,
or the auction man comes and takes everything
down to the last nail. Time to bungee and rope

the hatch closed so boxes and bags and hope
don't strew themselves down the highway.
Floor it. Leave. But that damn bird keeps sobbing,
that call trailing me down the driveway

after all of it. After everything. Stay. Stay.
That bird and its damnfool keening.
All of it. All the leaving.

Mown

under the moon tramps out
scythe lays bare the meadow
shrieking with vermin fled
the blade of his harrowing
scrape of steel on stone
field flora topple before him
dainty their fresh stems bleeding
straightened neatened up isn't that how
it's done isn't that history that's discovery
children barefoot nightgowned
dim imagos little moons shine pale
in all the windows witness to carnage
you're next he says you're next

Rebellion of the Things

The furniture insisted.

We'd thought each piece carefully chosen.
We'd thought all along they were ours.
They caught us and kept us,
first you and then when you
struggled against them to get yourself
free, and I moved to help you, then me.

Said one: I am a chair.
You must sit. And I sat. We were helpless,
both of us, you and then me.
We thought these demands at first kind of a joke.
We thought at first we would laugh.
It ended, we ended in tears, tears and chains.

Minimal, stainless, formally restrained,
the Sub-Zero towers athwart us;
door swinging open, by inches discloses
serried ridges of its pale maw.
The Prius joins in. We'd bought it
for its economy. And the ormolu clock
handed down from your great-aunt Bessie.

Now the knock-together desk, the sly one
missing a caster, grins and pops open
its swollen-stuck drawer to reveal
zip ties, staple gun, oh, unwinding lazily,
roll of duct tape. Flashing, the letter-knife.

Garden of Earthly Delights

One rogue Scarlet O'Hara peony
determined to be pink.
The irises outflagged by weeds.
Dependent from a sagging pole, the empty feeder,
its hummers lured away by neighbors.
Ivy chokes the turtle-boy fountain dry,
and the cracked drain beneath him gapes,
the drain out of which, last year, a black snake
periscoped for my inspection.
Tangle of wind chimes. Bench,
wrought-iron, bolted together with rust.
Glowering over all, the magisterial spadix
of the arum lily,
its bloated poison lips.

In Memory, the Woodthrush

Tangle of the chiming deep from thicket
off the road's curve, rushing
and thriving shadows underneath
four o'clock, silence rounding after.
Again farther off. Again til only
the coinage of echo remain.
Now just a dim cool imprint,
gold and silver jangling hidden forever
maybe where the sweet water fled
the time they stole our river,
spat out upon us ash, returned
our change in mud.

Salute to the Bluebird Café

To dawdle Main Street in the rain,
wipers bursting against the windshield,
browse my own reflection staring back
from deep in defunct plate glass windows
papered over. Fire Department Stew Sale!
Have You Seen This Cat? Worship With Us
This Sunday MARLA AND BILL "SON" CLYDE,
PASTORS. They sport matching pompadours.
To scuff along the sidewalk and go in,
slap of the screen door, burr of the fans.
Hunker around a thick-rimmed mug beneath the eye
of the paint-chipped elk across the street
outside the lodge. Tin-stamped ceiling stained
by seven decades of smokers, all
the lungs inside them stained the same.
To want to feel and fear to feel
the wad of gum fossilized beneath the table.
Rather than use the noisome restroom, hold it;
fail to read, through scratched-up clouded plastic,
the list of specials; not need to do so, already
knowing what they are. To order the lemon meringue,
edge-browned peaks stiff and gummy;
counter-side, to swivel the leatherette red stools,
wish for one last time a foaming Coke
drawn from a tap into a paper cone,
settled in a little metal stand.

Ornithomancer

The ovates sort, some eviscerate
sparrows, cranes, hawks, doves,
divine the stones and seeds.
The ones who stand by altars
when the eagle drops like thunder on the left,
Zeus, they whisper.

Patterns swifts or grackles make,
swerving fields or chimneys, are they random?
Iphigenia, tame canary down the mine,
augurs her own doom. Cassandra scries.
None listen; the crone, swaying on her tripod,
doles out riddles silver-etched under brass moon.

The gazelle springing

the way Witness leafs out in spite of everything,
even disappointment, into the heart of spring.

The addax of pure white, the saiga, the eland,
Animal made Joy, leaping to the heart of spring.

Turn of the year. I guzzle solitary wine
for these grim days. The earth drinks up the green
      heart: spring.

Ravished, I wander down these garden paths
      where thrush,
warbler, finch sing us back into the heart of
      spring.

Out of death unfolds life. Love's tender shoot
      must reach
to sun, must cleave, all clades, each to each their
      heartspring.

Stotting and lekking, the oryx, blackbuck, brocket
protect and mate from start to wanton heart of
      spring.

Alone at the verge I watch the herd ripple out
a river of savannah through the heart of spring.

Winter's dormant species "Jane." Rue, thrift,
      opening
reluctant sepal, petal. The freshet-heart. Spring.

The Bee Telephone 36

Acknowledgments

Thanks to the editors of the journals where the following were first published:

'The Bee Telephone'
An earlier version of this poem was first published in *So It Goes: The Literary Journal of the Kurt Vonnegut Museum/Library*, issue no. 5, 2016.

'Glyph'
This poem has been revised from a version published in *Poetry Quarterly*, Summer 2016 issue, p. 24.

'The comet, that hairy star'
This poem was first published in *The Broken City*, issue #30, 2022, p. 6.

'Slow Waking'
This poem was first published in *Eclectica*, April/May 2023.

'Penelope, Exasperated'
An earlier version of this poem, the featured poem for Nov. 28, 2022, was published on the poetry site *SWWIM Everyday*,
https://www.swwim.org/swwimeveryday/2022/11/28/penelope-exasperated

'Coming soon to skies near you'
An earlier version of this poem was published in *The Westchester Review*, Summer issue, 2022.

'Breughel and Babel'
This poem was published in *Southern Poetry Review*, issue 61:1 (fall 2023).

'Sell your soul to the Devil at the crossroads'
An earlier version of this poem was published in *Feral: A Journal of Poetry and Art*, #16, June 30, 2023.

The Bee Telephone 38

About the Poet

Jane Wiseman is a writer who splits her time between the Sandia Mountains of New Mexico and very urban south Minneapolis. Her poetry has appeared most recently in *Southern Poetry Review*, *Main Street Rag*, *Eclectica*, and other publications. A transplanted Southeasterner, Jane has lived all over the U.S. She holds an undergraduate degree from Duke University, an MA from the University of Illinois-Urbana, and a PhD from the University of Pennsylvania. She has taught at a number of colleges and universities.

Judge Steve Brisendine's Comments

The language in *The Bee Telephone* reeled me in from the outset. It challenges and unsettles in all the best ways. It covers vast territories of place and time and, even after repeated readings, I can't find a foot put wrong.

Whether mining veins of antiquity, chronicling the moment a dandelion launches its seeds into the night, or looking forward to some imagined end private or global, the poet's imagery is at once familiar and alien (the latter in a way which invites rather than repels).

This, from "I'm talking good news," perfectly encapsulates that winning dichotomy:

> *I'm talking close your windows, lock your doors. Here comes kudzu. The innocuous zucchini chaste beneath its leaf by day swells monstrous in the night. It beats down your door, menaces the dog, steals your changeling babies.*

I'm more than happy to make this chapbook my choice as this year's winner.

Steve Brisendine lives, works and remains unbeaten against *The New York Times* crossword in Mission, Kansas. He is the author of five collections of poetry, most recently *full of old books and silence* (Alien Buddha Press, 2024) and *Behind the Wall Cloud of Sleep* (Spartan Press, 2024). His work has appeared in *Modern Haiku, I-70 Review, Flint Hills Review* and other publications and compilations. He has no degrees, one tattoo and a deep and unironic fondness for strip-mall Chinese restaurants. In his spare time, he tries to make himself seem far more interesting than he actually is.

1st Finalist
2024
Jonathan Holden
Poetry Chapbook Contest

Hosted by

Choeofpleirn Press

These poems are about awe, about how the simplest moments of our lives are the most important—sharing stories with family in the car or on the boat, that first kiss with a future spouse "for no reason" (which he knows is actually the best reason). Most people don't realize until much later how important these quiet moments, these "bright whispers" are, but what makes Shrum's work so extraordinary is that he understands their reverence as he lives them.

Melissa Fite Johnson, author of *Midlife Abecedarian* and *Green*.

2nd Finalist
Jonathan Holden Poetry Chapbook Contest
2024

How do we shake the detritus from our memories? A geographic transplant, Rochelle Germond washes clean those memories she rediscovers before leaving those excavations behind to discover not only what can frighten her but also what gives meaning to this new location where "the wishbone we snap breaks evenly in half, / a sure sign that we will both receive our pleas."

James P. Cooper

Author of *Listening for Low Tide*
Honorable Mention for the Eric
Hoffer Book Award

Available at Amazon and
Choeofpleirn Press

Listening for Low Tide

Too much happens at ground level:
the kids selling candy or delivering
newspapers shortcut through the yard,
the neighbors' dogs blare their alarms
in unison, and teens, shielded by the heartbeat
of their music, speed down the street.

Two stories above the ground.
I welcome the afternoon sunlight
as it stretches across the rug,
my cat moving with it. From the opposite
window, the shadows cast by trees
overspread the ground, the sunlight only
hitting the treetops. Sound waves lap
against the building, the tide at its lowest
each night when the owl in the park
starts to hoot its presence.

Choeofpleirn Press
www.choeofpleirnpress.com
2024